COOL SCIENCE

Experiments with Heat and Energy

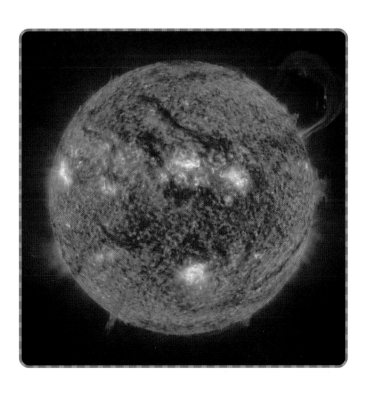

By Lisa Magloff

Gareth Stevens
Publishing

Please visit our Web site www.garethstevens.com. For a free color catalog of all our high-quality books, call toll free 1-800-542-2595 or fax 1-877-542-2596.

Library of Congress Cataloging-in-Publication Data
Magloff, Lisa.
    Experiments with heat and energy / Lisa Magloff.
       p. cm. -- (Cool science)
    Includes index.
    ISBN 978-1-4339-3450-6 (lib. bdg.) -- ISBN 978-1-4339-3451-3 (pbk.)
    ISBN 978-1-4339-3452-0 (6-pack)
    1. Heat--Experiments--Juvenile literature. 2. Heat transfer--Experiments--Juvenile literature.
    3. Thermodynamics--   Juvenile literature. I. Title.
QC256.M338 2010
536--dc22   2009041577

Published in 2010 by
Gareth Stevens Publishing
111 East 14th Street, Suite 349
New York, NY 10003

For Gareth Stevens Publishing:
Art Direction: Haley Harasymiw
Editorial Direction: Kerri O'Donnell

For The Brown Reference Group Ltd:
Editorial Director: Lindsey Lowe
Managing Editor: Tim Harris
Editor: Sarah Eason
Children's Publisher: Anne O'Daly
Design Manager: David Poole
Designer: Paul Myerscough
Production Director: Alastair Gourlay

Picture Credits:
Front Cover: Corbis: Bohemian Nomad Picturemakers (foreground); NASA: SOHO (background)
Title Page: NASA: SOHO
Shutterstock: James Doss 7t, Anastasiya Igolkina 4, Videowakart 7, Erwin Wodicka 6
All other images Martin Norris

Publisher's note to educators and parents: Our editors have carefully reviewed the Web sites that appear on p. 31 to ensure that they are suitable for students. Many Web sites change frequently, however, and we cannot guarantee that a site's future contents will continue to meet our high standards of quality and educational value. Be advised that students should be closely supervised whenever they access the Internet.

Manufactured in the United States of America
1 2 3 4 5 6 7 8 9   12 11 10

CPSIA compliance information: Batch #BRW0102GS: For further information contact Gareth Stevens, New York, New York at 1-800-542-2595.

Contents

Introduction

People are always comparing how hot things are. For example, Australia is hotter than Antarctica. A fire is hotter than an ice cube. The Sun is hotter than almost anything we can imagine. But what exactly is heat?

The Sun is the source of all the heat on Earth.

Scientists have puzzled over the nature of heat for hundreds of years. They have learned a lot about heat and how it works by doing experiments like the ones you will do in this book.

Everything in the universe is made up of tiny particles called atoms. There are many different kinds of atoms. They join up in many different combinations, called molecules. These molecules make up the stars in the sky, the rocks on which we stand, and even the cells, tissues, and organs that make up our bodies.

The atoms and molecules in an object are always on the move. As they move, these tiny particles bump into each other. Heat is this movement of atoms and molecules. When an object is hot, that means that the atoms and molecules in it are moving around very quickly and bumping into each other.

If you look at a burning match, you won't see it moving. But the atoms that make up the burning match are buzzing around all the time. So why does the match appear to stay still when its atoms and molecules are moving around? That is because the atoms move by a very small amount. They vibrate, which means they move around a fixed point. This vibration is fast—far too quick to see. But we can feel the vibrations as heat.

Making heat

There are lots of different ways to make heat. They all involve making the atoms and molecules in an object move around faster. If you hold an object over a flame, the atoms and molecules in the object start to move quickly. It gets hotter. When electricity flows through a copper wire, the copper atoms vibrate and the wire gets hot. As the space shuttle re-enters Earth's atmosphere, the air rubs against the surface of the spacecraft. The atoms and molecules that make up the body of the shuttle start to vibrate. The surface of the shuttle gets hotter.

Heat as energy

Heat is just one form of energy. There are many different forms of energy, from the chemical energy that is stored in a battery to the kinetic energy stored up in a moving object. Whatever form it comes in, energy is the ability to make something happen. For example, electrical energy can light up a lightbulb. Heat energy can make things happen, too. For example, it can melt solid objects such as ice cubes. It can also make the atoms and molecules in different substances rearrange themselves to make new substances.

BE SAFE!

The activities in this book involve lots of hot liquids, candles, and other sources of heat. Heat can be dangerous. You need to stand away from any heat source and hot objects. If you do need to handle hot things, always use oven mitts—even when you think the object has cooled. The experiments in this book are all safe if you follow the instructions very carefully in each one. If you are ever in any doubt about what to do, ask an adult to help you.

LEARNING ABOUT SCIENCE

Doing experiments is the best way to learn about science. This is the way scientists test their ideas and find out new information. Follow this good science guide to get the most out of each experiment in this book.

• Never begin an experiment until you have talked to an adult about what you are going to do.
• Take care when you do or set up an experiment, whether it is dangerous or not. Make sure you know the safety rules before you start work. Wear goggles and use the right safety equipment when you are told to do so.
• Do each experiment more than once. The more times you carry out an experiment, the more accurate your results will be.
• Keep a notebook to record the results of your experiments. Make your results easy to read and understand. You can make notes and draw charts, diagrams, and tables.
• Drawing a graph is a great way of presenting your results. Plot the results of your experiment as dots on a graph. Use a ruler to draw a straight line through all the dots. Reading the graph will help you to fill in the gaps in your experiment.
• Write down the results as you do each experiment. If one result seems different from the rest, you might have made a mistake that you can fix immediately.
• Learn from your mistakes. Some of the most exciting findings in science came from an unexpected result. If your results do not tally with your predictions, try to find out why.

What is temperature?

People describe how hot things are by talking about their temperature. Generally, it is hotter in the summer than it is in the winter. People say that the temperature is hotter in the summer than in the winter. But there is an important difference between heat and temperature. A bucket of water at room temperature contains more heat energy than a cup of boiling water, even though the temperature of the water in the cup is higher. You can test this by pouring the cup of boiling water and the bucket of water over some snow. The bucket of water will melt much more snow than the cup of boiling water because it has more heat energy.

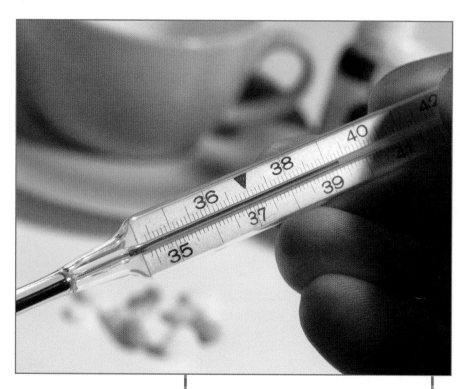

You can use a thermometer to take the temperature of your body.

Heat changes

Objects change when they get hot. As an object gets hotter, the atoms and molecules vibrate more. The space between them gets bigger, which is why the object gets bigger. Atoms are so small that it is impossible for you to see this happening with your eyes, but engineers need to think about it when they build bridges and other structures. They leave small gaps between different sections of the bridge to allow for the changes that take place in materials during hot conditions. When the weather is hot, the metals expand and the bridge gets bigger. Without gaps, the bridge sections would press into each other. The bridge would then collapse.

Sometimes heat can produce spectacular changes. With enough heat, you can make the atoms in a metal vibrate so hard that they break apart and start sliding around each other. When this happens the metal melts and turns from a solid into a liquid. If you add more heat, the atoms in the molten metal vibrate so much that the metal will eventually turn into a gas—just as liquid water turns into steam. At this point, the molten metal has boiled to become a gas.

Different objects melt and boil at different temperatures because the forces that hold them together are weaker and stronger. The forces between the atoms in a metal are stronger than the forces between the molecules in water. That is why water boils at a much lower temperature than metals.

Movement of heat

Heat always moves from hot objects to cooler objects. There are three main ways heat moves: conduction, convection, and radiation.

Conduction: When you put a metal spoon in a cup of boiling water, the spoon will start to feel very hot very quickly. The boiling water makes the atoms in the spoon vibrate, and these vibrations pass down the spoon to the handle. This is called conduction. Materials such as metals are very good at conducting heat.

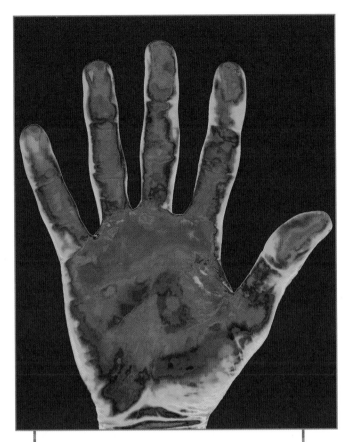

A thermal image of a hand glows in bright colors to show the heat given off by our bodies. Our eyes cannot see this heat, but special cameras can reveal it.

GEYSERS

For the experiment on page 24, you will build your own working model of a geyser. Geysers shoot hot water and steam out of the ground with tremendous force. Geysers occur when water touches molten (liquid) rock deep underground. The water collects in channels of rock. The water at the bottom of the channel is under pressure from the water above. At high pressure, water boils at a much higher temperature than the usual 212°F (100°C). The water at the top of the channel is under less pressure so it boils away. This makes the pressure drop at the bottom of the column. The water there then boils over suddenly, producing a violent eruption of steam and hot water at the surface.

Other materials such as plastics do not conduct heat very well. They are called insulators.

Convection: Heat spreads through the air and in liquids by convection. When air or a liquid heats up from below, it rises and pushes cooler air or liquid above out of the way. The cooler air or liquid sinks, heats up again, and then rises. This is a convection current. It consists of rising warm air (or liquid) and sinking cool air (or liquid).

Radiation: Heat can also move by radiation. Hot objects emit a form of light, called infrared radiation, that people cannot see. The hotter an object is, the more infrared radiation it emits. This is how the heat from sunlight warms up our planet.

"Old Faithful" in Yellowstone National Park, Wyoming, erupts almost every hour. Each time, it shoots out enough water to fill 385 bathtubs.

Testing Temperature

Goals

1 Test the ability to sense changes in temperature using your hands.

2 Experiment with different materials to find out how well they conduct heat.

LEVEL of Difficulty   Hard   Medium   Easy

What you will need

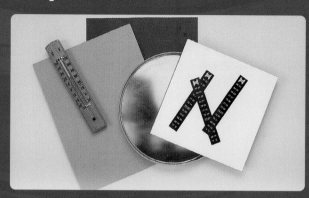

- thermometer
- three liquid-crystal thermometer strips
- test materials: card, ceramic tile, glass, metal, plastic, Styrofoam, and wood. The materials should all have a flat surface larger than your hand.

1 Leave the materials on a table for about an hour. Lay your hand on each material, one at a time, for about 3 seconds. Which material feels coldest?

2 Compare different materials by using both hands, one on each material. Does one hand feel hotter than the other?

SAFETY TIP!
Do not use glass with sharp edges because you might cut your hand.

8

LIQUID CRYSTALS

A liquid-crystal thermometer is a plastic strip containing a special liquid in a series of thin, clear pockets. The liquid is made of long, spiral molecules. As the temperature rises, the spiral molecules squeeze together like a spring. The liquid changes color. Different colors represent different temperatures. A number printed on the pocket also lights up to show the temperature.

3 Arrange the materials in order, from cold to warm, depending on how they feel.

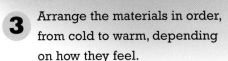

TROUBLESHOOTING

Why did the materials get warmer while I was doing the experiment?

If you leave your hand on the surface for too long, heat from your hand will warm up the object and change your results. Touch each object quickly and wait a minute or two before you touch it again. This will give the object time to return to room temperature.

4 Lay out a liquid-crystal thermometer on the surface of each material. Measure its temperature.

5 Use a room thermometer to measure the temperature of the room. Compare it to the temperature of each material. Are they the same?

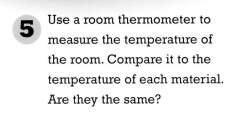

Measuring Conduction

What you will need

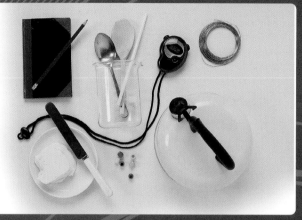

- butter
- beads
- butter knife
- wooden spoon
- straw
- length of copper wire 15 inches (37cm) long
- metal spoon
- glass bowl or beaker
- hot water
- stopwatch
- notebook and pencil

Goals

1 See how different materials conduct heat.

2 Learn the difference between a conductor and an insulator.

LEVEL of Difficulty Hard Medium Easy

2 Stick a bead onto the blob of butter.

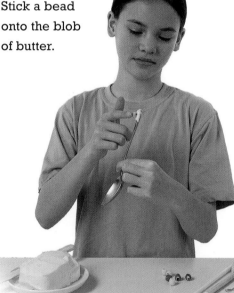

1 Put a blob of butter on the end of one of the items you are testing (wooden spoon, metal spoon, straw, and copper wire).

REPEAT YOURSELF!

Repeat the experiment several times. Each time, try to do the experiment in exactly the same way. Use the same amount of butter, put the blob of butter in the same place on each object, put them in the same place in the beaker, and boil the water each time. Your results will not be exactly the same every time, but they should be close to each other. Then change something to see if you get a different result. This is how scientists do experiments when they are testing a theory.

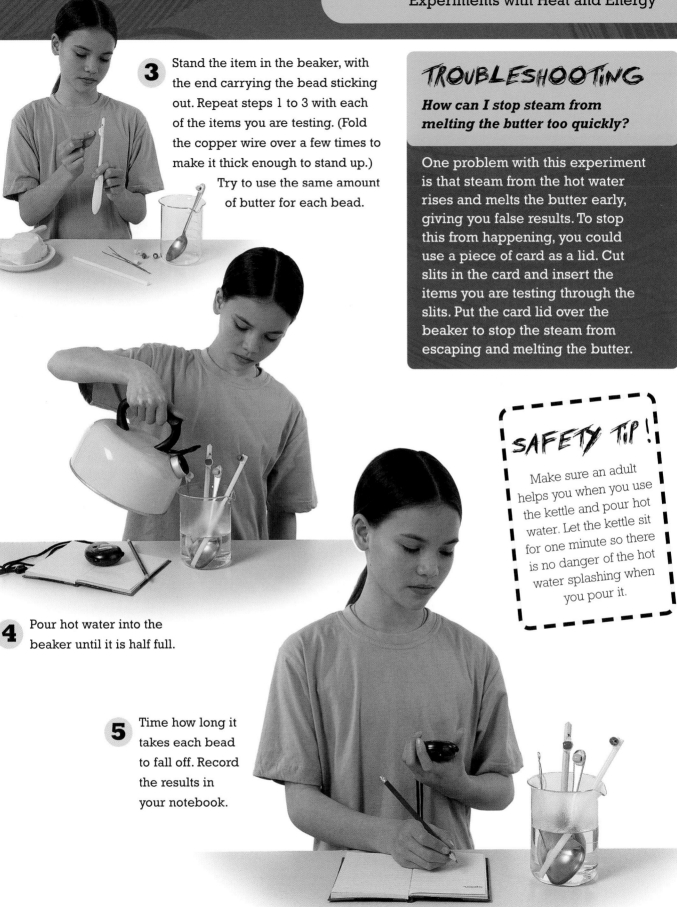

3 Stand the item in the beaker, with the end carrying the bead sticking out. Repeat steps 1 to 3 with each of the items you are testing. (Fold the copper wire over a few times to make it thick enough to stand up.) Try to use the same amount of butter for each bead.

SAFETY TIP!

Make sure an adult helps you when you use the kettle and pour hot water. Let the kettle sit for one minute so there is no danger of the hot water splashing when you pour it.

4 Pour hot water into the beaker until it is half full.

5 Time how long it takes each bead to fall off. Record the results in your notebook.

Hot Rod

Goals

1 Find out how copper pipe expands and contracts.

LEVEL of Difficulty — Hard · Medium · Easy

What you will need

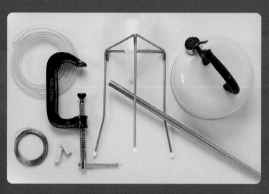

- copper pipe, 3 to 6 feet (0.9 to 1.8m) long
- 2 plastic tubes, 2 feet (0.6m) long. The plastic tube should fit snugly into or over the end of the copper pipe and the funnel.
- clamp
- 2 small blocks of smooth wood
- tripod
- funnel
- bucket
- 4-inch (10-cm) length of wire, or a paper clip
- hot water
- cold water

SAFETY TIP !

Always ask an adult before using hot water. An adult can help you boil the water and pour it into the tubes.

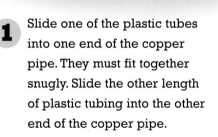

1 Slide one of the plastic tubes into one end of the copper pipe. They must fit together snugly. Slide the other length of plastic tubing into the other end of the copper pipe.

2 Put the two blocks of wood under the copper pipe. Space them out so that the pipe sits steadily on the work surface. Clamp the pipe and one of the blocks to the work surface.

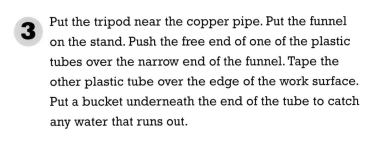

3 Put the tripod near the copper pipe. Put the funnel on the stand. Push the free end of one of the plastic tubes over the narrow end of the funnel. Tape the other plastic tube over the edge of the work surface. Put a bucket underneath the end of the tube to catch any water that runs out.

4 Bend the wire or paper clip into an L-shape. Put the wire between the copper pipe and the unclamped wooden block. The long part of the "L" should stick straight up. Make sure the wire is sticking out past the block.

5 Pour hot water into the funnel. Ask an adult to help you, because the water will be close to boiling. Remember to keep your hands away from the copper pipe. It will become hot, too.

TROUBLESHOOTING

What if the wire slips instead of turning when the pipe is hot?

Put a small piece of card between the wood and the wire. You can also help keep the wire in place by wrapping a rubber band around the wood and the copper pipe.

6 What happens to the wire when you pour the hot water through the copper pipe? Immediately pour cold water through the pipe. What happens to the wire now?

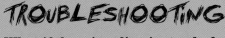

Make a Thermos

What you will need

- aluminum foil
- 2 small jars with lids
- sticky tape
- scissors
- Styrofoam
- warm water in a jug
- large jar with a lid
- 2 thermometers

Goals

1. Slow down heat transfer.
2. See how insulation works.
3. Build your own thermos to keep a liquid hot for as long as possible.

LEVEL of Difficulty

 Hard Medium Easy

SAFETY TIP!

Ask an adult to help you when you are using hot water from the faucet.

2 Put a small piece of Styrofoam in the bottom of the large jar.

1 Wrap two layers of foil around one of the small jars (shiny side facing inward). Hold them in place with sticky tape.

3 Measure the temperature of the warm water.

4 Pour a cup of warm water into each small jar. Put the lids on both jars.

TROUBLESHOOTING

What does it mean if the water temperature was the same in both jars at the end of the activity?

If the water at the start of the activity is close to room temperature, then you might not notice much change in temperature. It will still be at room temperature in both jars at the end of the activity. Make sure you use water from the hot-water faucet.

5 Stand the small jar with foil on the Styrofoam in the large jar. Put the lid on the large jar. Leave the second small jar of water on the work surface.

6 After ten minutes, measure the water temperature in both small jars. Which one contains the warmest water?

DIFFERENT GAS

You can replace air in the large jar with carbon dioxide (CO_2). Ask an adult to put a small candle in the large jar and light it just before you put the small jar in. Put the lid on. The candle will burn all the oxygen in the jar and then go out, leaving CO_2 in the jar. What difference does this make to your results?

Convection Tank

Goals

1 Create a convection current in water.

2 Understand how heat moves by convection through a liquid or gas.

LEVEL of Difficulty
 Hard
 Medium
 Easy

What you will need

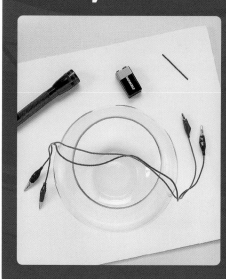

- lead from a mechanical pencil
- fish tank
- 6V battery
- cool water
- large piece of white posterboard
- 2 electrical leads with alligator clips at both ends
- flashlight

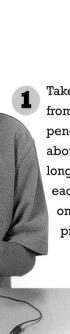

1 Take a piece of lead from a mechanical pencil. It should be about 2 inches (5cm) long. Clip one end of each electrical lead onto each end of the piece of lead.

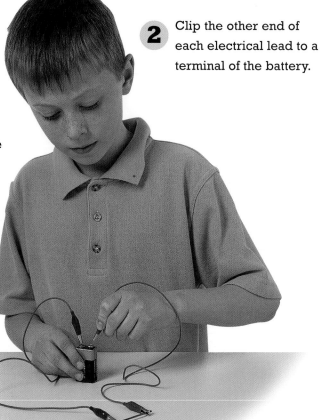

2 Clip the other end of each electrical lead to a terminal of the battery.

TROUBLESHOOTING

Why didn't the water move around in the bowl?

Try using a 12V battery and a thicker piece of lead. Ask an adult to remove the thick lead rod from the inside of a C battery. Make sure your flashlight beam is narrow and strong and that the room is completely dark.

3 Fill the tank with cool water. Place the lead into the water so that it hangs horizontally in the middle of the bowl. Make sure the lead does not touch the sides of the bowl.

4 Turn off the lights. Shine your flashlight through the tank so that the movements of the water show up on the posterboard behind the tank. See what happens.

MORE CONVECTION

Another way to see convection currents is to fill a glass bowl with vegetable oil. Set the bowl on two bricks a few inches apart. Light a small candle. Put it under the bowl between the two bricks. Add a few drops of food coloring to the oil. The food coloring will reveal the convection currents as the oil heats up.

5 If you cannot darken the room, you can still observe the currents by grinding black pepper into the bowl. The light flakes of pepper will move with the current.

Measuring Food Energy

What you will need

- small metal can
- large metal can
- weighing scales
- water
- thermometer
- notebook and pencil
- cork stopper
- sewing needle
- metal tray
- safety matches
- metal skewer
- small bag of cheese puffs, marshmallows, or shelled peanuts

Goals

1 Find out how much energy there is in your favorite foods.

2 Compare the amount of energy in different foods.

LEVEL of Difficulty

 Hard Medium Easy

1 Ask an adult to remove both ends of the large can and the top of the small can with a can opener. Ask him or her to punch two holes opposite each other near the tops of both of the small and large cans. Ask the adult to punch several holes around the base of the large can.

2 Put the small can on the scale. Set the scale to zero. Pour half a cup of water into the can. Record the weight (in kilograms). Since you set the scale to zero with the can on it, your reading will show the weight of the water.

SAFETY TIP!

Take care when you pick up the cans after the holes have been punched. The edges will be sharp. The cans could also get hot during the experiment. Do not pick them up until they have cooled.

3 Let the water reach room temperature. Measure the water temperature with the thermometer. Write down the temperature.

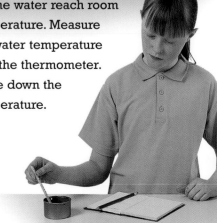

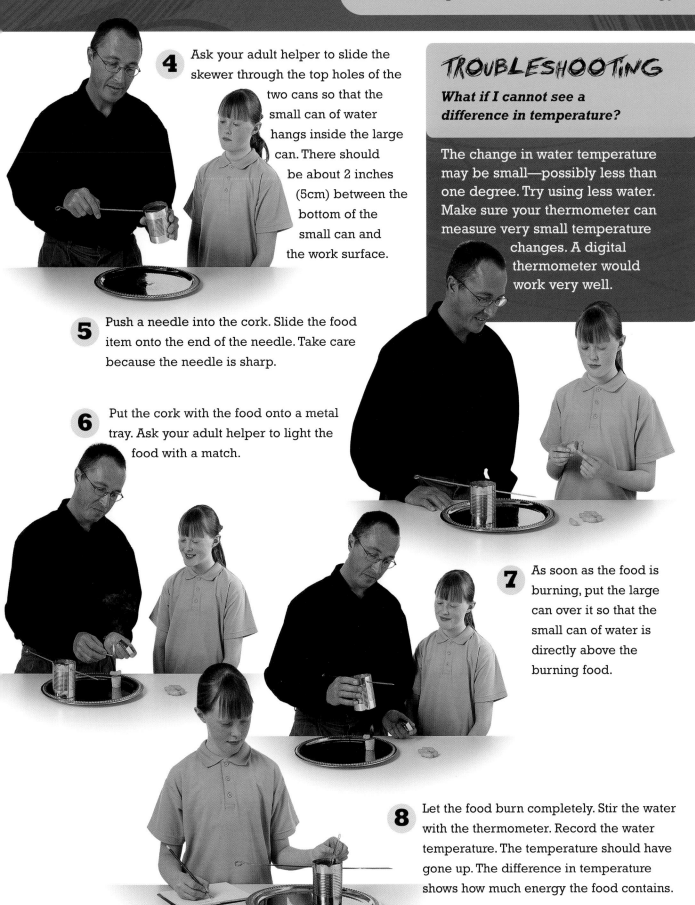

4 Ask your adult helper to slide the skewer through the top holes of the two cans so that the small can of water hangs inside the large can. There should be about 2 inches (5cm) between the bottom of the small can and the work surface.

5 Push a needle into the cork. Slide the food item onto the end of the needle. Take care because the needle is sharp.

6 Put the cork with the food onto a metal tray. Ask your adult helper to light the food with a match.

TROUBLESHOOTING

What if I cannot see a difference in temperature?

The change in water temperature may be small—possibly less than one degree. Try using less water. Make sure your thermometer can measure very small temperature changes. A digital thermometer would work very well.

7 As soon as the food is burning, put the large can over it so that the small can of water is directly above the burning food.

8 Let the food burn completely. Stir the water with the thermometer. Record the water temperature. The temperature should have gone up. The difference in temperature shows how much energy the food contains.

19

Slice Some Ice

Goals

1 See how pressure can affect the melting point of ice.

2 Make water refreeze by reducing pressure.

What you will need

- plastic bottle full of water
- steel fork
- aluminum foil
- tripod
- heavy book or weight
- thread or string
- ice cube

1 Lay the fork over the tripod. Weigh it down with a heavy book. Make sure the fork cannot move.

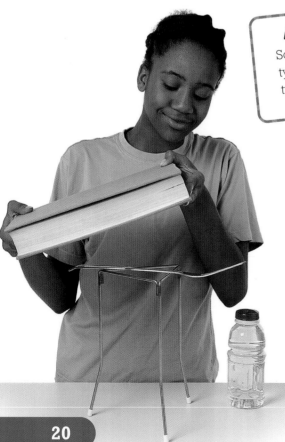

ELEVEN TYPES OF ICE
Scientists have identified 11 different types of crystalline ice. The different types form at different temperatures and pressures.

2 Tie a loop of string or thread around the neck of the bottle so that it supports the bottle's weight. Wrap it around a few times to make it secure.

3 Fold the foil into a small square. Put it over the tines of the fork. Put the ice cube onto the foil.

COLD OR HOT?

Frostbite occurs when your body is exposed to freezing temperatures for too long. The heat moves from your body to the cold air. If enough heat is lost, skin cells start to die. Hands and feet are vulnerable to frostbite because they have a large surface area through which to lose more heat. They are also farthest away from warm blood being pumped from the heart.

4 Put the loop of string over the top of the ice cube so that the bottle is hanging from the ice cube. Watch what happens.

5 Lift up the bottle after the thread has passed part of the way through the ice cube. Notice anything strange about it?

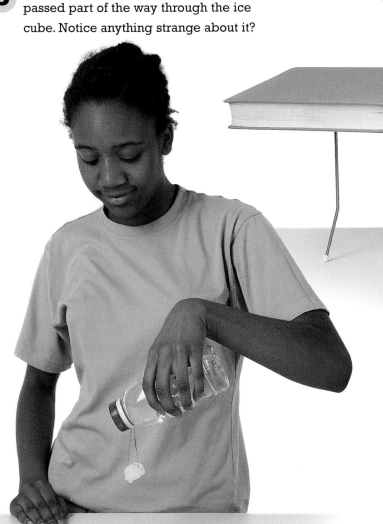

TROUBLESHOOTING

What if the ice cube melts before the thread can cut all the way through it?

This problem can be avoided by setting up the experiment in the refrigerator. You may need to take out a few shelves to fit it in, so ask permission first.

Solar Oven

What you will need

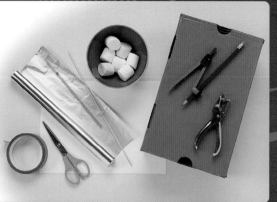

- shoebox or other long, narrow box
- compass and pencil
- scissors
- card
- aluminum foil
- sticky tape
- hole punch
- bendy straw
- wooden skewer
- marshmallows
- a sunny day

Goals

1 See how the Sun radiates heat.

2 Use solar radiation to cook food.

LEVEL of Difficulty Hard Medium Easy

1 Use the compass to draw two semicircles on the sides of the shoebox in the middle of the long edges.

2 Cut out the two semicircles.

3 Bend a piece of card into the two semicircles. Mark each side of the card to show where it fits into the semicircles. Remove the board. Cut the card to size.

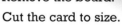

4 Stick aluminum foil on one side of the card. Make sure the shiny side is facing out. Try not to wrinkle the foil too much. You want it to be as smooth as possible.

SAFETY TiP !

Solar ovens can heat up to around 275°F (135°C). That is hot enough to cook food and kill germs in water. Cooking time in your solar oven will be twice as long as your home oven. You should allow half an hour in the Sun for the oven to preheat. Measure the temperature of any meat you have cooked in the oven using a cooking thermometer. Do not eat meat that is under 180°F (82°C).

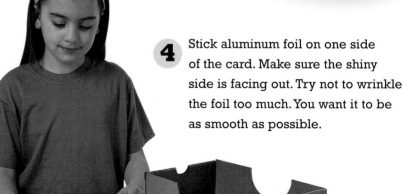

5 Fit the foil-covered card into the semicircles, shiny side up. Tape it onto the box, starting at the center and working toward the edges.

6 Cut out two card rectangles. Punch a hole in the center of each one, 1 inch (2.5cm) from the end. Tape the card rectangles to the sides of the box. Make sure the holes are at the top of the box on either side of the foil curves.

TROUBLESHOOTING

What if my solar oven does not get hot enough to cook food?

Solar ovens work best on clear, sunny days. Do not use them too late in the afternoon. The Sun may be too low in the sky to heat up the oven. You might want to move the oven as the food heats so that it catches the most Sun. Try making the foil curve larger or smaller to reflect more sunlight.

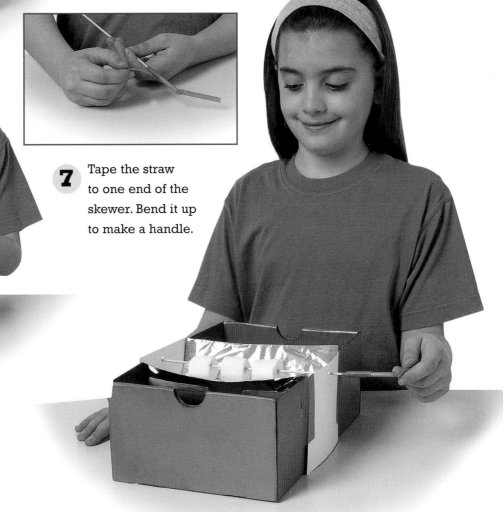

7 Tape the straw to one end of the skewer. Bend it up to make a handle.

8 Push the skewer through one of the punched holes. Thread marshmallows onto the skewer. Push the skewer through the other hole so that it is supported by the card rectangles.

9 Put the oven out in the Sun. Keep an eye on it to make sure it is not in the shade. Regularly turn the handle so that your marshmallows cook evenly.

Gushing Geyser

Goals

1 Build a working model of a geyser.

2 See how pressure affects the boiling point of water.

3 Find out about the relationship between heat and pressure.

LEVEL of Difficulty

 Hard Medium Easy

What you will need

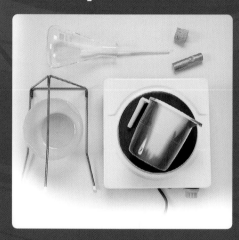

- heatproof plastic container
- heatproof plastic tube about 15 inches (38cm) long
- plumber's putty
- tripod
- hot plate
- one-hole rubber or cork stopper that fits in the mouth of the flask
- boiling flask or a heatproof glass jar with a narrow neck
- pouring jug and water

SAFETY TIP!

Ask an adult to help you when you do this experiment. The water spouting out of the geyser will be hot, so make sure you stand well away from the spray. Wait until the reaction is finished before you turn off the hot plate. Make sure you let the water cool down before cleaning up.

1 Ask an adult to cut a hole in the bottom of the plastic container. It should be big enough for the plastic tube to fit through.

2 Push the tube through the hole. It should poke up a few inches into the container but not be higher than the rim of the container. Seal the hole on the inside of the container using plumber's putty.

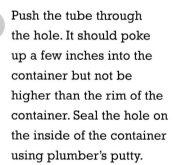

3 Push the other end of the tube through the stopper.

4 Place the tripod over the hot plate. Fill the flask halfway with water. Put the flask on the hot plate but do not turn it on yet. Put the stopper into the flask. The bowl should rest on the tripod.

TROUBLESHOOTING

Where should I set up my geyser?

Set up the experiment away from any electrical appliances. Ask an adult to check that the hot plate's electrical cord is not cracked or missing insulation. Put the hot plate on a flat, even surface. Lay newspaper or an old tablecloth over the surface to soak up any spills.

GEYSER CITY

Yellowstone National Park in Wyoming contains 400 of the world's 700 geysers, including Steamboat Geyser—the world's tallest erupting geyser. Major eruptions can reach more than 350 feet (100m), and they are unpredictable!

5 Pour cold water into the plastic container until the top of the tube is covered with 1 inch (2.5cm) of water.

6 Ask an adult to turn on the hot plate. Stand back.

25

Cloud in a Jar

What you will need

- large glass jar
- measuring cup
- water
- candle
- rubber glove

Goals

1 Understand the relationship between pressure, volume, and temperature.

2 Use pressure to create a cloud in a jar.

LEVEL of Difficulty

 Hard   Medium   Easy

2 Turn a rubber glove inside out. Put a floating candle inside the jar. Ask an adult to light the candle. After a few seconds, blow the candle out. Stretch the glove over the neck of the jar to cover it completely.

SAFETY TIP!

Take care when you are working around a flame. You could burn yourself.

1 Pour about one-quarter of a cup of water into the bottom of the jar.

3 When the flame has gone out, put your hand in the glove. Push your hand into the jar.

TROUBLESHOOTING

What if the cloud does not appear in the jar?

Make sure that the seal between the glove and the jar is very tight. You could wrap a rubber band around the neck of the jar to make the seal very tight. Also check your rubber glove—it might have a hole in it.

4 Clench your fist. Pull your hand up while holding the jar steady with the other hand. Look into the jar as you pull up. You should see a cloud form in the jar. The cloud should disappear when you stop pulling up.

5 Repeat the experiment, but this time put the glove over the jar while the candle is still burning. When the flame has gone out, put your hand into the glove and pull it out of the jar as before. What happens inside the jar this time?

VAPOR TRAILS

Water vapor is an invisible gas, but we can sometimes see it in the air as it turns from a gas into a liquid. The vapor trails behind a jet airplane are an example. Jet fuel turns into hot gases when it burns, including water vapor. As the vapor blasts out of the jet, it turns into water and ice as it meets the cold air outside. This forms the long, thin, cloudlike vapor trails behind the jet airplane.

Cool Science

Making Ice Cream

Goals

1 Lower the temperature of ice.

2 See how materials change state to form new materials.

3 Make some tasty ice cream.

LEVEL of Difficulty
 Hard Medium Easy

What you will need

- 2 cups of milk or half-and-half
- 1 sandwich-size Ziploc bag
- ¼ cup of sugar
- 2 teaspoons of chocolate sauce or vanilla extract
- 4 cups of ice
- ½ cup of salt
- 1 large Ziploc freezer bag
- masking tape or duct tape

1 Pour the milk or half-and-half into the small Ziploc bag. Add the sugar.

2 Add the chocolate sauce or vanilla extract. Close the bag.

3 Squeeze the bag with your hand. Mix the ingredients well.

SAFETY TIP! Wash your hands before you do this activity to stop germs from spreading.

4 Put 2 cups of ice and ¼ cup of salt in the large bag. Add another 2 cups of ice and ¼ cup of salt. Put the small bag inside the large bag. Push it down so that it is covered in ice.

EXPERIMENT WITH FLAVORS

Make exciting flavors by adding crushed up candy bars to the milk before you seal the small bag. Use food coloring to make your ice cream more colorful.

5 Close and seal the large bag. Shake the bag for about 15 minutes. You might need mittens to keep your hands warm!

6 After the 15 minutes are over, open the bags, and enjoy your ice cream.

TROUBLESHOOTING

What if the ice cream doesn't freeze?

The first thing to do is seal the bags again and shake for a few more minutes. You could use less milk to make the ice cream. Simply cut all the measurements in the recipe in half. The ice cream will then freeze faster. Try adding more ice and salt to the large bag. Stir them to make sure the salt is well mixed with the ice.

Glossary

atoms: the tiny building blocks of all objects. Atoms are made up of protons, electrons, and neutrons.

battery: a device that changes chemical energy into electrical energy

boiling: turning from a liquid into a gas

boiling flask: a glass container used to heat substances

conduction: in heat, when the atoms and molecules vibrate in a substance so that heat energy passes through it

conductor: a substance, such as metal, through which heat moves very easily

convection: heat transfer in a liquid or gas. The atoms and molecules in the cool parts of a liquid or gas pack together tightly and they sink. The atoms and molecules in the warm parts of a liquid or gas are more loosely packed and they rise.

electricity: the flow of electric power or charge. Electricity powers many of our machines, such as televisions, radios, and computers.

energy: the ability of something to make things happen. For example, a ball moving through the air has energy because it could smash a window.

frostbite: when parts of the body such as the hands and toes freeze because it is so cold

geyser: a boiling spring that regularly shoots out a column of hot water and steam into the air

heat: energy that transfers between two objects or an object and its surroundings because they are a different temperature

infrared: an invisible form of radiation

insulator: a substance, such as plastic, through which heat does not move very easily

liquid: one of the states of matter. Liquids have a fixed volume but no shape, so they take the shape of their container.

melting: turning from a solid into a gas

molecules: a group of atoms joined together by chemical bonds

pressure: the amount of force acting on a surface

radiation: any form of energy that is moving through space. Radiation can be visible light or infrared radiation, for example.

Styrofoam: a very light plastic filled with air bubbles

temperature: a measure of the heat in something

terminal: in batteries, the places where electricity flows to and from

thermometer: an instrument used to measure temperature

thermos: a container that is used to keep liquids hot or cold by slowing down the transfer of heat between the inside and outside

vapor: another word meaning "gas." For example, water vapor is steam.

volume: the amount of space an object occupies

Further Information

BOOKS

Fullick, Ann. *Turning Up the Heat: Energy*. Mankato, MN: Heinemann-Raintree, 2005.

Mahaney, Ian F. *Heat*. New York: Rosen Publishing, 2007.

Parker, Steve. *Heat and Energy*. New York: Chelsea House Publications, 2004.

Tocci, Salvatore. *Experiments with Energy*. New York: Children's Press, 2004.

Tocci, Salvatore. *Experiments with Heat*. New York: Children's Press, 2003.

WEBSITES

www.explorit.org/science/energy.html

www.energyquest.ca.gov

www.eere.energy.gov/kids/

Index

DEC 1 4 2010